LIGHTHOUSES OF NEW YORK

A Guidebook and Keepsake

Help Us Keep This Guide Up to Date

Every effort has been made by the authors and editors to make this guide as accurate and useful as possible. However, many things can change after a guide is published—phone numbers change, facilities come under new management, etc.

We would love to hear from you concerning your experiences with this guide and how you feel it could be improved and be kept up to date. While we may not be able to respond to all comments and suggestions, we'll take them to heart and we'll also make certain to share them with the authors. Please send your comments and suggestions to the following address:

The Globe Pequot Press
Reader Response/Editorial Department
P. O. Box 480
Guilford, CT 06437

Or you may e-mail us at:

editorial@GlobePequot.com

Thanks for your input, and happy travels!

LIGHTHOUSES SERIES

LIGHTHOUSES OF NEW YORK

A Guidebook and Keepsake

Bruce Roberts and Ray Jones

INSIDERS' GUIDE®

GUILFORD, CONNECTICUT
AN IMPRINT OF THE GLOBE PEQUOT PRESS

INSIDERS' GUIDE®

Copyright © 2006 by Bruce Roberts and Ray Jones

Text design by Schwartzman Design, Deep River, CT
Map design and terrain by Stephen C. Stringall, Cartography by M.A. Dubé
Map © Morris Book Publishing, LLC.
All photographs, unless otherwise credited, are by Bruce Roberts.

Library of Congress Cataloging-in-Publication Data
Roberts, Bruce, 1930–
    Lighthouses of New York : a guidebook and keepsake / Bruce Roberts and Ray Jones. –
    1st ed.
        p. cm. – (Lighthouses series)
    ISBN 0-7627-3967-3
    1. Lighthouses–New York–History. 2. Lighthouses–New York–Guidebooks. I. Jones, Ray,
    1948– II. Title. III. Series: Lighthouses series (Globe Pequot Press)

VK1024.N7R63 2005
387.1'55'09747–dc22

                                                                    2005013626

Manufactured in China
First Edition/First Printing

CONTENTS

LIGHTHOUSES OF NEW YORK

ONTARIO

VERMONT
- Montpelier
- 302
- 89
- 4

NEW HAMPSHIRE

MASSACHUSETTS
- 7

CONNECTICUT
- Hartford
- 1
- 95

NEW YORK
- Albany
- Hudson City
- Saugerties
- Roundout Creek
- 9
- 20
- 88
- 44
- 48
- 9W
- 209
- 206

Atlantic Ocean
- Race Rock
- Montauk Point
- Orient Point
- Little Gull Island
- Shinnecock Bay
- Horton Point
- Old Field Point
- Fire Island
- Eaton's Neck
- Stepping Stones
- Execution Rocks
- New York
- Stony Point
- Jeffrey's Hook
- Coney Island
- Statue of Liberty
- Robbins Reef
- Staten Island

NEW JERSEY
- 206

PENNSYLVANIA
- 6
- 15
- 219
- 522

Lake Ontario
- Ogdensburg Harbor
- Rock Island
- Tibbetts Point
- East Charity Shoal
- Selkirk (Point Ontario)
- Oswego West Pierhead
- Sodus Point
- Charlotte-Genesee
- Rochester
- 11
- 104
- 81
- 20
- 390
- 490

Lake Erie
- Thirty Mile Point
- Fort Niagara
- Buffalo Main (Point Gratiot)
- Barcelona
- Dunkirk (Point Gratiot)
- Buffalo
- Toronto
- 90
- 20
- 20A
- 62
- 11

Toronto

100 Miles

100 KM

INTRODUCTION

The United States of America is a highly commercial nation, part industrial and part agrarian. The growth and prosperity of the United States has depended on safe navigation of waters leading to its busy port cities, none of them more important than those in New York. As a result, lighthouses have been a major concern for Americans and for New Yorkers right from the first.

A farmer and a lifelong landlubber, George Washington rarely went to sea, but he was a friend and enthusiastic promoter of commerce and, therefore, of lighthouses. Before the revolution, Washington had visited New York and noticed there a number of fine locations for navigational beacons. Among these were the future sites of the Horton Point Light near Southold and of the grand old Montauk Point Light at far eastern end of Long Island.

Washington's interest in lighthouses would continue throughout his careers as a military man and politician. In 1789, as president, Washington urged the very first U.S. Congress to pass legislation taking federal control of all coastal lighthouses. At that time the nation had only a few scattered lights to mark more than 2,000 miles of coast.

U.S. Lighthouse Service

Anxious to encourage commerce, President Washington recognized that the new nation's system of coastal lights was woefully inadequate. Under pressure from the president, Congress made lighthouses a priority and, in one of its very first official acts, created the U.S. Lighthouse Service. In one form or another, the service would survive for more than 150 years, right up until 1939 when the U.S. Coast Guard took responsibility for the nation's navigational aids. By that time more than one thousand fine lighthouses marked the Atlantic and Gulf coasts in the East, the Pacific and Bering Sea coasts in the West, and the shores of the Great Lakes in the Midwest.

A century and a half earlier, however, when the Lighthouse Service was in its infancy, the number of operational lights was pitifully small, including only eleven functional lights. Scattered along the coast from Portsmouth, New Hampshire, to Charleston, South Carolina, these beacons all dated from colonial times, and most had been allowed to fall into a sad state of disrepair by the financially strapped states that now owned them. New York had only one lighthouse, and interestingly enough, it was in New Jersey. The Sandy Hook Light, built in 1764 with New York money at behest of New York City merchants, stood at the end of a long peninsula about 8 miles from Staten Island. The light—its tower is now the oldest in the United States—marked the entrance to the Lower New York Bay and pointed the way to the Hudson River and the bustling wharves of New York City.

Despite the fact that the Sandy Hook Light had been built by New Yorkers and was of great benefit to them, the State of New Jersey laid claim to the structure following the Revolutionary War. This led to an almost comical court battle between the two states, characterized by a great deal of puffing and overblown rhetoric. The dispute dragged on for years and was only finally resolved when, after the framing of the U.S. Constitution, the new federal government stepped in and took control of the light. Along with it, the government assumed responsibility for coastal beacons throughout the country. With funds appropriated by an often reluctant Congress, the newly established U.S. Lighthouse Service launched an ambitious construction program that would add a dozen major maritime towers to the nation's system of shore lights within a decade. Among these were lighthouses at Cape Henry, Virginia (completed in 1791); Portland Head, Maine (1791); Tybee, Georgia (1791); Seguin, Maine (1795); Bald Head, North Carolina (1796); Montauk Point, New York (1797); Baker's Island, Massachusetts (1798); Cape Cod, Massachusetts (1798); Cape Hatteras, North Carolina (1798); Ocracoke, North Carolina (1798); Gay Head, Massachusetts (1799); and Eaton's Neck, New York (1799).

Perhaps appropriately, this initial burst of lighthouse construction was completed shortly before George Washington died during the final weeks of 1799. The old general missed by only seventeen days witnessing the beginning of the nineteenth century and, with it, the opening of a whole new era of expansion and prosperity. As a revolutionary, leader of the Continental Army, framer of the Constitution, and the nation's first president, Washington had done more than almost any American to make this new and optimistic age possible. Among his most important contributions, however, was one that is not frequently recognized: his insistence on an efficient system of lights for America's coasts and navigable inland waters.

A Tale of Two Lighthouses

America's lighthouses have made navigation easier and safer, but they have also served as symbols, both profound and practical. While welcoming others to our shores, they have signaled our strength announcing our intention to play a prominent role on the world stage. Some lighthouses are, in fact, so closely linked to our nation's history that they are quite rightly considered national monuments. This is the story of two such beacons, one at the far eastern end of Long Island and the other at the gates of New York City.

For many of the millions of immigrants who came to America in search of opportunity and a better life, the first glimpse of their new home was the beacon of a distant lighthouse. It may have been the

Located near the entrance to Long Island Sound, the Race Rock Light stands atop an artificial island of stone.

Ronald J. Foster

Boston Lighthouse, the Cape Hatteras Lighthouse on North Carolina's Outer Banks, the Cape Henry or Cape Charles Lighthouses at the entrance of the Chesapeake Bay, or any one of dozens of other prominent coastal lights. But for many, perhaps even for most, immigrants it was the beacon of the Montauk Point Light, built in 1797 at the far end of Long Island that first welcomed them to America.

The prominent bluff at the far eastern extremity of Long Island reminded early European settlers of the hump in a turtle's back, so they called the place Turtle Hill. But the unpretentious name belies the importance of this strategic point of land. Long before the arrival of the white man, the first beacons burned on the hill known to Indians as Womponamon. According to legend, leaders of the powerful Montauk tribe lit signal fires at the summit of the hill to call their chiefs and warriors to council. The vessels guided by this light were dugout canoes carved from the trunks of large trees. Some say that the British also banked bright fires on the hill. During the Revolutionary War several of King George's ships lay off Montauk Point in order to blockade Long Island Sound. The fires served these warships as beacons.

After the war the new U.S. government recognized that it must follow the example of the British and the Indians before them. Such a significant and dangerous headland could not be left unmarked, and President George Washington himself ordered construction of a lighthouse on Montauk Point. It was to be an expensive project. Contractor John McComb of New York submitted a low bid of $22,300 to dig foundations, haul sandstone, and build the tower and two-story keeper's dwelling. At a time when lighthouses elsewhere were being built for as little as $2,000, this was a hefty price. Land for the light station had been purchased for only a little more than $250. But McComb gave the country its money's worth. He built the lighthouse like a fortress, with a foundation 13 feet deep and walls 7 feet thick at the base. As a consequence, the Montauk Point Light still stands after two centuries of blasting by Atlantic storms. McComb had also been the contractor for a lighthouse erected in 1791 on Cape Henry in Virginia. The tower he built there, though unused for more than a century, stands to this day.

The Montauk Point Light continues to guide ships more than 200 years after its lamps first burned. Not all of the sailors who have seen the light, however, have reached port safely. Storms have driven many vessels against the beaches near Montauk, usually with disastrous results. Some ships got permanently stuck in the sand, others broke in half and sank, and a few "melted like a lump of sugar" in the raging surf. More than a century ago, local residents told a correspondent for *Harper's New Monthly* magazine about "how a ship was driven ashore one wild night . . . how brave men gathered to the rescue; how the crew, one after another dropped into the sea, some of them being saved from the jaws of the angry waves; of a mother washed ashore, dead, clasping a babe in her arms; the wild figures of the wreckers on that dark, stormy night of horrors, lit up by a great fire of drift-wood. . . . "

For many decades the lamps of the lighthouse at Montauk Point burned whale oil. By the mid-1850s whalers had decimated the world's whale population. Seeing that it could no longer count on a regular supply of whale oil, the Lighthouse Service switched to lard oil as a fuel here and elsewhere. Later many lighthouse lamps, including those at Montauk, burned kerosene.

Lamp Beside the Door

America's most widely known symbol of freedom is the Statue of Liberty. Striking a bold pose on the island near the entrance to New York City Harbor, the statue has welcomed visitors and immigrants to America for more than a century. With its bright lantern thrusting more than 300 feet above the water, the statue was intended to serve as a lighthouse. For many years it was recognized as an official harbor light, useful to vessels moving up and down the Hudson River or headed for the city wharves.

Known officially as the "Statue of Liberty Enlightening the World," it was the dream of a nineteenth-century French historian named Edouard de Laboulaye, a passionate admirer of American political institutions. Laboulaye raised money for the project in France, hired Frederic Auguste Bartholdi to design the statue, and, when it was completed in 1884, presented it to the United States as a gesture of French–American friendship. The dismantled statue arrived in New York in enormous packing crates. Reassembled on twelve-acre Bedloe Island, now known as Liberty Island, it was dedicated in 1886 by President Grover Cleveland.

Now universally recognized as a symbol of freedom, the Statue of Liberty once served as a lighthouse. William G. Kaufhold

The statue appears today almost exactly as it did more than a century ago, but it has required continual maintenance and care. During its centennial in 1986, it received a multimillion-dollar renovation, which included replacement of the 1,600 wrought-iron bands that hold the copper skin to its iron frame. The statue weighs approximately 450,000 pounds. From her heel to the top of her head, the lady stands 111 feet tall. Her toenails are more than a foot across. Her most heroic quality, however, is not her extraordinary size but, rather, the very powerful idea she represents. A symbol recognized the world over, she is freedom's lighthouse. Perhaps the Emma Lazarus poem engraved on a tablet at the statue's base conveys this message best. It reads:

> Not like the brazen giant of Greek fame,
> With conquering limbs astride from land to land;
> Here at our sea-washed, sunset gates shall stand
> A mighty woman with a torch, whose flame
> Is the imprisoned lightning, and her name
> Mother of Exiles. From her beacon-hand
> Glows world-wide welcome; her mild eyes command
> The air-bridged harbor that twin cities frame.
> "Keep ancient lands, your storied pomp!" cries she
> With silent lips. "Give me your tired, your poor,
> Your huddled masses yearning to breathe free,
> The wretched refuse of your teeming shore.
> Send these, the homeless, tempest-tost to me,
> I lift my lamp beside the golden door!"

How to Use This Guide

In one way or another all of New York's lighthouses are closely linked to our nation's history, and each of them has a fascinating story to tell. New York can boast more than thirty standing light towers and all are historic. In *Lighthouses of New York* you will learn their histories and enjoy their stories, as you discover how, when, and why these maritime skyscrapers were built. This book takes you to each accessible lighthouse and to some that simply can't be reached. It also takes a loving backward glance at New York's lost lights, beacons that once shined bright but were snuffed out long ago.

As you'll see, the book is divided into three sections: Long Island: Race Point to Eaton's Neck, New York City and the Hudson: Staten Island to Hudson City, and The Great Lakes: Rock Island to Barcelona. Within each section lighthouses are presented in geographic order, just as they would appear on a map. This arrangement should make it easier to plan your own New York lighthouse outings—so should the directions, telephone contacts, and other travel information included at the end of each listing.

Under normal circumstances, you should be able to visit the most attractive and historic lighthouses in one or another of the sections mentioned above in a single long weekend excursion. To help you select the lighthouses you want to visit, individual listings include advice in the form of simple symbols: 🏛 for lighthouses that are especially historic—most of them are, 🚪 for lighthouses that are accessible—more than a few are not, 📷 for visitor-friendly lighthouses that are frequently open to the public and feature museums or similar attractions, and 📷 for lighthouses that make great pictures—most of them are quite photogenic. A fifth symbol 📐 indicates those lost lighthouses, historic towers that, unfortunately, no longer exist. For added convenience, every listing also includes an easy-to-read summary of key information on the lighthouse: location, date the light was established, height of the tower, type of optic, current status, characteristic, range, and elevation of the beacon, and for all active lights, the precise latitude and longitude of the beacon.

We hope you enjoy your New York lighthouse adventure.

CHAPTER ONE
LONG ISLAND: RACE POINT
TO EATON'S NECK

Among the largest and most recognizable geological features in
New York, if not all of North America, is Long Island. Built up
over millions of years as rivers, glaciers, and ocean currents
deposited sand, silt, clay, and gravel atop a bed of metamorphic
rock, Long Island extends more than 120 miles eastward from the
mouth of the Hudson River to the sandy bluffs of Montauk Point.
On a map or chart, the island looks something like a giant lobster
claw, an appropriate image since it has been crushing the hulls of
ships for centuries. The low and nearly featureless headlands often
cannot be seen at all from the water, and mariners who steer too
close risk running aground on a beach or ensnaring their vessels in
the shoals and shallows just offshore. Standing astride some of the
busiest sea lanes in the world, Long Island represents a formidable
obstacle.

To help mariners stay on course and keep a safe distance from
the island, its shores are well marked with navigational lights. Not all
of these lights emanate from lighthouses. Some are mere channel
markers, while others are "lesser" lights placed on small, iron-skeleton
towers or atop concrete fog-signal structures. Others are traditional
lighthouses, that is, they have a tower with lantern at the top and a
residence for a keeper.

Perhaps most historic of the Long Island lighthouses are those
at Eaton's Neck, first lit in 1799, Montauk Point, established in
1797, and Horton's Point, built in 1790. Among the oldest standing
lighthouses in the United States, these venerable maritime towers
were completed and placed in operation during the presidential
administrations of George Washington and John Adams. All three
remain in use today more than two centuries after they first started
guiding mariners.

Horton Point Light in Southold has celebrated more than 200 Christmases.

Ronald J. Foster

MONTAUK POINT LIGHT

President George Washington personally ordered construction of the Montauk Point Light at the strategic far-eastern tip of Long Island. Washington's successor, John Adams, was in office when the project was completed in 1797. The sandstone tower and adjacent two-story dwelling cost $22,300, a sizable fortune at the time. The young U.S. government got its money's worth, however, as the still operational 110-foot tower has passed its two-hundredth birthday.

The station's flashing white light, produced nowadays by an aero-marine beacon, shines out toward the open Atlantic from a height of 168 feet above the water. Its guidance is heartily welcomed by seamen, none of whom want to come near the killing sands and surf of Montauk, where ships have been known to "melt away like butter."

TO SEE THE LIGHT: The light is in Montauk State Park at the end of Route 27. Since 1987, when the last resident keepers left the station, the dwelling has served as a maritime museum, where visitors may view fascinating historical exhibits and a marvelous array of Fresnel lenses and other lighting devices. Contact Montauk Point Lighthouse Museum, Box 943, Montauk, NY 11954; (631) 668–2544; www.montauklighthouse.com. To the west in Cedar Point County Park, off Route 114, is the granite block Cedar Island Lighthouse (1868), abandoned since 1934.

Location: Montauk

Established: 1797

Tower height: 110 feet

Elevation of the focal plane: 168 feet

Optic: Modern

Status: Active

Characteristic: Flashes every 5 seconds

Range: 18 miles

Position: 41° 04' 15
          71° 51' 26

Note: More than two centuries of continuous service

Montauk's airport-style rotating lamps produce a flash every 5 seconds.

RACE ROCK LIGHT

Although it is positioned only about 5 miles from Watch Hill, Rhode Island, and less than 8 miles from New London, Connecticut, the Race Rock Light is actually located in the state of New York. It stands on a high stone pier near where three state boundaries come together just off the tip of New York's Fishers Island.

A long list of ships have come to grief on Fishers Island and the nearby coasts of Connecticut and Rhode Island, but Race Point Reef itself is particularly vicious. During the 1700s and early 1800s, the reef sank ships at a rate of nearly one per year. In 1829 alone the reef claimed at least eight ships, and there likely were other wrecks that went unreported.

In 1838 Congress appropriated $3,000 to build a lighthouse on Race Rock, but this sum was so pitifully inadequate that construction was put on hold indefinitely. Meanwhile the carnage continued. Perhaps the worst disaster occurred in 1846, when the passenger steamer *Atlantic* slammed into Race Point Reef, with a loss of fifty-seven lives. Despite this calamity, it was not until 1869 that Congress finally appropriated a more realistic sum of $90,000 to build the lighthouse.

But even this would prove insufficient. Before the Race Rock light station was complete, its price tag would balloon to $278,716, placing it among the most expensive lighthouses ever built. It was also one of the most remarkable engineering feats of its era.

Construction of a lighthouse in the open waters of Long Island Sound proved a daunting task. To attempt it, federal officials employed F. Hopkinson Smith, a well-known construction engineer. Smith in turn hired as his foreman Thomas Scott, a sharp-tongued former ship's captain whom he described as a "bifurcated sea dog."

First a pier had to be constructed in 13 feet of often turbulent water. Smith and Scott tried building an artificial island. Enormous loads of broken rocks and boulders—10,000 tons in all—were poured onto the site, but the strong currents swept away the fill almost as fast as boats could deliver it. Frustrated, Smith and Scott resorted to the much slower and more expensive method of having divers lay cement on the sea bottom. This process took nearly two years but eventually produced a mass of concrete some 9 feet thick and 69 feet in diameter. Upon this pad they were able to construct a stone pier.

The job was still far from finished. Progress was impeded by storms, ice, sunken supply barges, exhausted funding, appropriation delays, and the death of two workmen in separate accidents. It was

Location: Near Fishers Island

Established: 1879

Tower height: 45 feet

Elevation of the focal plane: 67 feet

Optic: Modern

Status: Active

Characteristic: Flashes red every 10 seconds

Range: 16 miles

Position: 41° 14' 37 72° 02' 49

Note: An extraordinary feat of lighthouse engineering

not until February 21, 1879–more than eight years after work began–that a keeper climbed the steps of the tower and lit the lamps for the first time.

Built of large granite blocks, the two-story Race Rock Light stands on a massive stone pier rising almost 30 feet above high water. The attached square tower places the light approximately 67 feet above the surface of Long Island Sound. The automated light alternates between red and white flashes and can be seen from 14 miles away.

TO SEE THE LIGHT: Race Rock Light can be reached only by water, but you can see it from Watch Hill, Rhode Island, and several points along the Connecticut coast. Ferries operating between New London, Connecticut, and Block Island or Orient Point on Long Island often pass within sight of the station. For schedule and fares call (401) 783–4613.

Ronald J. Foster

LITTLE GULL ISLAND LIGHT

ocated in Long Island Sound between Fishers Island and Plum Island, the Little Gull Island Light has guided mariners since the early 1800s. However, the station has changed significantly during its two centuries of existence. The granite tower that marks the island today dates to 1867 when it replaced an earlier, less substantial structure. The mighty hurricane of 1938 severely damaged the station, and after the light was automated in 1978, the Coast Guard demolished the dwelling. Although it stands alone now, the old tower continues to guide mariners with its flashing light.

TO SEE THE LIGHT: Off limits to the public, the Little Gull Island Light is best seen from the water. For cruises that pass it, call the East End Seaport Museum at (516) 477–2100.

Location: Long Island Sound

Established: 1806

Tower height: 81 feet

Elevation of the focal plane: 91 feet

Optic: Modern

Status: Active

Characteristic: Flashes twice every 15 seconds

Range: 17 miles

Position: 41° 12' 23
72° 06' 25

Note: Fine example of a coffeepot tower

Al Pochek

SHINNECOCK BAY LIGHTHOUSE

The historic Shinnecock tower was demolished in 1948 to make room for a parking lot.

National Archives

Location: Shinnecock

Established: 1858

Tower height: 170 feet (original)

Elevation of the focal plane: 75 feet (skeleton tower)

Optic: Modern (skeleton tower)

Status: Deactivated 1931 and destroyed 1948

Characteristic: Flashes twice every 15 seconds (skeleton tower)

Range: 9 miles (skeleton tower)

Position: 40° 50' 31 (skeleton tower) 72° 28' 42 (skeleton tower)

Note: Was one of America's tallest brick lighthouses

S everal generations of mariners looked to the soaring Shinnecock Bay tower and its powerful beacon to guide them along the dangerous shores of eastern Long Island. The station served from shortly before the Civil War until 1931 when its light was deactivated and replaced by an automated beacon on a skeleton tower. The latter marker remains in use, but the grand old brick lighthouse was destroyed after World War II to make way for a Coast Guard administrative center. Local residents, who could not imagine gazing skyward without seeing the big tower, had struggled for years to convince Coast Guard officials to preserve it, but to no avail. In 1948, a team of laborers spent two weeks sawing through the base of the giant cylinder and, finally, down it came like a mighty redwood.

TO SEE THE LIGHT: All that remains of Shinnecock Lighthouse are some rubble and the old oil house at the Coast Guard base.

ORIENT POINT LIGHT

Just off the northeastern tip of Long Island, a deep but narrow passage called Plum Gut links several heavily trafficked bodies of water, including Long Island Sound and Gardiners Bay. Strong currents make navigating any part of the Gut a tricky business. But a helmsman's chief concern is Oyster Pond Reef, a deadly ledge lurking just beneath the surface of the water and extending fully one third of the way across the waterway.

To mark this unseen menace, in 1896 the Lighthouse Board approved construction of a caisson-type tower in the open water at the far end of the reef. The Orient Point Light took two years to build and was not operational until 1899. It cost $30,000, about six times the original estimate for the project. To protect the structure from high waves driven by gales, the builders piled hundreds of tons of broken stone around its base. Painted brown at the top and white at the bottom, the cast-iron tower was not particularly handsome. It was soon given the nickname "Coffee Pot" by mariners who passed regularly through Plum Gut.

The station's first keeper was N.A. Anderson, a Norwegian immigrant. He was married, but because his isolated light station was considered too small and dangerous for a woman, his wife lived in the town of Orient on Long Island. Anderson served for twenty years in the Coffee Pot at a salary of $50 a month. Now unmanned and automated, the Orient Point Light guides maritime traffic with a white flash every five seconds. The tower stands 64 feet above the water, and its light can be seen for 17 miles.

TO SEE THE LIGHT: You can see the Orient Point "coffeepot" Light from the ferry landing at the end of Route 25. The church-and-steeple-style Plum Island Lighthouse (1869), which is no longer active, is visible to the east of the landing. The ferry that provides passage to New London, Connecticut, offers an excellent view of both lighthouses. On the way across the sound, passengers also get a look at the impressive 80-foot, granite-block Little Gull Island Light (1867). For schedules and fares call (860) 443–5281.

Location: Orient Point

Established: 1899

Tower height: 45 feet

Elevation of the focal plane: 64 feet

Optic: Modern

Status: Active

Characteristic: Flashes every 5 seconds

Range: 17 miles

Position: 41° 09' 48
72° 13' 24

Note: Fine example of a coffeepot tower

HORTON POINT LIGHT

In 1757, during the French and Indian War, a young military officer from Virginia paused atop one of the high bluffs of Southold, New York, and gazed thoughtfully down onto Long Island Sound. He had come here to see firsthand a notorious dangerous stretch of coast known locally by the forbidding name "Dead Man's Cove" because so many ships wrecked on its sands. The Virginian told his companions that someday a lighthouse would be built on the very spot where he was standing. His name was George Washington, and many years later, in 1790, while serving as the nation's first president, he would commission the lighthouse himself.

In June 1990 the Horton Point Light celebrated the 200th anniversary of its commissioning. The event, attended by dignitaries and many friends of the old lighthouse, was doubly significant. On that same day the light was restored to active service after standing dark for fifty-eight years, the Coast Guard having decommissioned the lighthouse in 1933.

The Horton Point Light seen today was built on the bluffs during the mid-1850s. In June 1857, a century after Washington first visited the place, the whale-oil lamps were lit and the third-order Fresnel lamp began to throw light out over the Sound.

From 1903 to 1904 Stella Prince served as keeper of the Horton Point Light. Born and raised in the lighthouse itself, she was the daughter of an earlier keeper. Appointed by President Theodore Roosevelt, she was one of only a few women ever to receive an official appointment as a lighthouse keeper.

TO SEE THE LIGHT: From Route 48 in Southold, turn north onto Sound View Avenue and follow the signs to Horton Point Lighthouse Museum. The tower houses this excellent museum filled with nautical artifacts; call (631) 765–5500. A few miles east, at the entrance to Orient Harbor, is the Long Beach Bar Lighthouse (1993), a replica of the original 1870 screw-pile lighthouse that burned to the ground in 1963. It can be seen from several points in the town of Orient as well as from nearby Shelter Island.

Location: Southold

Established: 1790

Tower height: 58 feet

Elevation of the focal plane: 103 feet

Optic: Modern

Status: Active

Characteristic: Flashes green every 10 seconds

Range: 14 miles

Position: 41° 05' 06
72° 26' 44

Note: Tower houses a nautical museum

OLD FIELD POINT LIGHT

Location: Stony Brook

Established: 1823

Tower height: 35 feet

Elevation of the focal plane: 74 feet

Optic: Modern

Status: Active

Characteristic: Alternates red and green every 12 seconds

Range: 14 miles

Position: 40° 58' 37 73° 07' 07

Note: Light now serves as the Old Field Village Hall

This lighthouse marks one of several fingers of land that stretch northward to menace shipping in Long Island Sound. The granite combination tower and dwelling seen here at present was completed in 1868. It replaced an earlier, though similar, structure that had served since 1823. The station was deactivated in 1933, but was placed back in service in 1991.

TO SEE THE LIGHT: The light, owned by the Village of Old Field, is closed to the public. It can be seen from Old Field Road north of Setauket. A better view is from aboard the Bridgeport (Conn.) to Port Jefferson ferry; call (631) 473–0286 or (203) 335–2040.

Al Pochek

What Is a Lighthouse?

The term "lighthouse" has been applied to a variety of buildings and beacons constructed for the purpose of guiding ships. Early coastal beacons were mostly open fires set blazing on top of a tall building or at the summit of a hill or sandy bluff. Usually these were operated by port authorities, maritime guilds, or local merchants who hoped to promote commerce. The "keepers" they hired or, in places where slavery was common, forced to tend the fires, might or might not have lived near the place they worked. As more and more beacons were established on islands or in other remote locations, the residences of keepers and the towers became more closely identified. By the seventeenth or eighteenth centuries, the notion of a lighthouse as a dwelling with a light tower had become more or less fixed.

About a century ago, the U.S. Lighthouse Service saw the need to define some of the terms it used. The service defined "lighthouse" as a "light station where a resident keeper is employed." Lighthouses usually included one or more residences, a light tower, a storage facility, and sometimes a separate building to house foghorn machinery. To help the keepers feed themselves and their families, the property often had a garden patch, chicken coop, and even a barn for cows.

For all practical purposes, the profession of lighthouse keeper is extinct in America. Not only have keepers vanished, but the Lighthouse Service itself is now only a memory. In 1939 the government handed responsibility for buoys and beacons over to the U.S. Coast Guard. The Coast Guard then began to automate the nation's shore lights. One by one America's fine old lighthouse keepers' residences were boarded up or torn down. By the end of the 1970s, most New York lighthouses had been automated.

One of the last New York lighthouses to lose its keeper was the remote Race Rock Light.
Ronald J. Foster

Ronald J. Foster

FIRE ISLAND LIGHT

I n 1850 the freighter *Elizabeth* struck a shoal and sank almost in the shadow of the Fire Island Light, which had guided shipping along the south shore of Long Island for almost twenty-five years. Sea captains had long complained that the 74-foot light tower was too short to give adequate warning of the shoals. The tragic loss of the *Elizabeth* along with most of her crew brought a general public outcry to which Congress quickly responded. The entire Lighthouse Service was soon under close scrutiny, and a Lighthouse Board was formed to revamp the nation's sadly deteriorated system of navigational lights.

The Lighthouse Board approved the construction of a new brick tower more than twice as high as the original. When completed in 1858, it stood 168 feet above the island sands. Focused by a first-order Fresnel lens, the light could now warn mariners as far as 24 miles from the coast.

Long ago, the station's flashing white beacon earned it the nickname "Winking Woman." The lighthouse stopped winking in 1974, when the station was decommissioned. Rapidly deteriorating, the abandoned lighthouse was on the point of being demolished when a local preservation society came to the rescue. Happily, it has been restored and relighted, and it is now a prime seashore attraction. The residence now serves as a visitor center and maritime museum.

TO SEE THE LIGHT: From Route 27A take the Robert Moses Parkway onto Fire Island and follow signs to parking for the light. For additional information or tours contact the Fire Island Lighthouse Preservation Society, Box 4640, Captree Island, NY 11702; (631) 661–4876.

Location: Fire Island

Established: 1826

Tower height: 168 feet

Elevation of the focal plane: 187 feet

Optic: Modern

Status: Active

Characteristic: Flashes every 7.5 seconds

Range: 24 miles

Position: 40° 37' 57 73° 13' 07

Note: New York's tallest and most impressive maritime tower

William G. Kaufhold

EATON'S NECK LIGHT

Location:	Asharoken
Established:	1799
Tower height:	73 feet
Elevation of the focal plane:	144 feet
Optic:	Fresnel (third order)
Status:	Active
Characteristic:	Fixed white
Range:	18 miles
Position:	40° 57' 14 73° 23' 43
Note:	Structure changed little in over two centuries

Eaton's Neck Light near Asharoken on Long Island is one of only a handful of surviving eighteenth-century light towers. Established to guide ships into Huntington Bay and through the western reaches of Long Island Sound, it was completed in 1799.

To supervise construction of the tower and dwelling, the government hired John McComb, who also served as contractor for the Montauk Point and Cape Henry lights. Obviously, McComb built structures intended to last, as these two towers and the 73-foot octagonal tower at Eaton's Neck still stand after two centuries of storm, rain, and wind. The Eaton's Neck Light received substantial repairs and renovation in 1868. Otherwise, it has required only minor patching and fixing and remains essentially the same structure today that McComb built in 1799.

Originally equipped with only a simple oil lamp, the lantern displayed a weak light visible from just a few miles out into the sound. Eventually, the station was fitted with an Argand lamp and reflector system designed by Winslow Lewis. The highly polished, 13-inch reflectors provided a more powerful light, but the Lewis system was decidedly inferior to the Fresnel lenses manufactured by the French. For many years Fifth Auditor Stephen Pleasonton of the Treasury Department resisted adoption of the Fresnel system because of the high cost of the hand-polished glass lenses— and, some would say, because of his preference for Lewis. By the time Eaton's Neck Light received its third-order Fresnel in 1856, Pleasonton was no longer head of the U.S. Lighthouse Service.

Since this area is frequently blanketed by fog, early Eaton's Neck keepers spent many hours striking the station's bell. During the 1868 renovation the bell was replaced by a siren. In 1904 an automated foghorn took over the task. Although the station is still used as a dwelling by Coast Guard personnel, the light itself is automated. Since the tower stands on a bank nearly equal to its own height, the light shines from a lofty 140 feet above the waters of the sound.

TO SEE THE LIGHT: Despite its historic nature and presence on the National Register of Historic Places, the Eaton's Neck Light station is not readily open to visitors. You can get special permission to visit, however, by contacting the U.S. Coast Guard Station, Eaton's Neck, Northport, NY 11768; (631) 261–6959.

William G. Kaufhold

Ronald J. Foster

EXECUTION ROCKS LIGHT

The light station marks a rugged island and navigational obstacle in the western reaches of Long Island Sound. The island's rather grim name dates to the Revolutionary War when, according to legend at least, British troops chained condemned prisoners here and left them to be drowned by the flooding tide. The rocks proved no less a threat to ships than to hapless patriots, for more than a few unfortunate navigators have lost their way in the fog and slammed into the low, almost invisible outcropping. To save ships and lives, the U.S. Lighthouse Service established a light station here in 1850. The granite tower and attached dwelling remain standing, although the residence is no longer in use. Automated in 1978, the light is powered by batteries recharged with solar panels.

TO SEE THE LIGHT: Accessible only by boat, the light is visible from a number of points in New Rochelle and along the shores of Long Island Sound.

Location: Off New Rochelle

Established: 1850

Tower height: 60 feet

Elevation of the focal plane: 62 feet

Optic: Modern (solar powered)

Status: Active

Characteristic: Flashes every 10 seconds

Range: 15 miles

Position: 40° 52' 41
73° 44' 16

Note: Marks a rugged island in Long Island Sound

The oil house and radio beacon pictured below were destroyed in a 1992 storm. Bob and Sandra Shanklin, The Lighthouse People

STEPPING STONES LIGHT

Bob and Sandra Shanklin, The Lighthouse People

Location: Off Kings Point

Established: 1877

Tower height: 38 feet

Elevation of the focal plane: 46 feet

Optic: Modern

Status: Active

Characteristic: Green occulting every 4 seconds

Range: 8 miles

Position: 40° 49' 28
73° 46' 29

Note: Marks a rugged island in Long Island Sound

For more than one-and-a-quarter centuries this offshore light station has guarded a dangerous shoal obstructing the waters of Long Island Sound just off Kings Point. Even today, mariners ignore at their peril the warning of its green, occulting light. The old sentinel also marks the far eastern reaches of the sound where it narrows dramatically and navigators must take great care. The station consists of a square brick tower attached to the front of a rather blocky residence. No keeper has lived or worked full time here since the light was automated in 1969.

TO SEE THE LIGHT: The light is accessible only by boat. However, it can be seen from the Throgs Neck Bridge.

CONEY ISLAND LIGHT

A blue-collar light if ever there was one, the sturdy, steel-skeleton tower on Coney Island was assigned the task of guiding New York City garbage barges to their watery dumps several miles out into the Atlantic. Built in 1890, the light also guided hulking iron freighters to Coney Island loading docks.

The 68-foot Coney Island tower consists of a central steel cylinder topped by an enclosed platform, which, in turn, is crowned by the gallery and lantern room. The entire structure is braced by four steel legs arranged to form a pyramid. Originally, the Coney Island Light was the rear member of a pair of range lights marking a safe channel for the garbage scows. The front range light was taken out of service shortly before the turn of the twentieth century, but the rear range light remains in service to this day. It displays a flashing red light.

TO SEE THE LIGHT: From Interstate 278 follow the Prospect Parkway and Ocean Parkway to Coney Island. The light is on Surf Avenue between Forty-sixth and Forty-seventh streets in the community of Seagate. The fourth-order Fresnel lens, which focused the Coney Island Light until the station was automated in 1989, is on display in the South Street Seaport Museum in lower Manhattan. Another attraction of this famous maritime museum is the Lightship Ambrose (Number 87), launched in 1907. Call (212) 748–8600.

Location: Brooklyn

Established: 1890

Tower height: 70 feet

Elevation of the focal plane: 75 feet

Optic: Modern

Status: Active

Characteristic: Flashes red every 5 seconds

Range: 16 miles

Position: 40° 34' 36
74° 00' 42

Note: Steel-skeleton tower

William G. Kaufhold

CHAPTER TWO
NEW YORK CITY AND THE HUDSON:
STATEN ISLAND TO HUDSON CITY

The story of the New York City and Hudson River lights begins at a lighthouse that is not even located in New York. Instead, it stands on a sandy New Jersey peninsula near the entrance to the Lower New York Bay. There on the evening of June 11, 1764, a keeper trudged up the steps of the recently completed Sandy Hook Light and lit its lamps for the first time. Today, more than two centuries later, the light at the very top of the old tower still burns each night. It is not America's first lighthouse—that honor goes to the Boston Light, established in 1716 and destroyed by the British in 1779—but it is the nation's oldest still standing and operating navigational aid.

Although located in New Jersey, the Sandy Hook Light was known for many years as the New York Lighthouse. Indeed, it was built and paid for by New Yorkers. Weary of losing commerce to better-marked harbors at Boston and elsewhere, a group of New York merchants petitioned their colonial council for a lighthouse. The New York Assembly then held a lottery to raise money and hired Isaac Conro to build a tower near the mouth of the Hudson. To defray the costs of maintenance and pay the keeper's salary, the assembly levied a tax of twenty-two pence per ton on ships arriving at the Port of New York.

When completed, Conro's handiwork was described as follows: "This House is of an Octogan Figure, having eight equal sides; the Diameter of the Base 29 feet; and at the Top of the Wall 15 feet. The Lanthorn is 7 feet high; the Circumference 15 feet. The whole Construction of the Lanthorn is Iron; the Top covered with Copper. There are 48 Oil Blazes. The Building from the Surface is Nine Stories; the whole from Bottom to Top 103 feet." The dimensions of the tower remain roughly the same today.

After the Revolution the Sandy Hook Light precipitated a different sort of war. Since the light was located in New Jersey but owned by New York, the two states fell into a heated dispute over control of the station. The verbal and legal squabbling continued for years, until the U.S. government finally put an end to the conflict in 1791 by taking control of the light along with other, previously state-owned light stations throughout the country.

When the Lighthouse Board began its massive effort during the 1850s to rebuild and modernize America's outdated light stations, inspectors were sent to see if the Sandy Hook tower would need to be replaced. Their report on the board is a compliment to the work done by Conro almost a century earlier: "The tower at Sandy Hook main light was constructed in 1764 under royal charter, of rubblestone, and is now in a good state of preservation. Neither leaks nor cracks were observed in it. The mortar appeared to be good, and it was stated that the annual repairs upon this tower amount to a smaller sum than in towers of any of the minor lights in the New York District."

Although the light remained structurally sound, the board decided to make one key improvement: to replace the old lens and reflector optic with a state-of-the-art, third-order Fresnel lens. Amazingly, that same lens still shines in the Sandy Hook tower, its beacon guiding ships to wharves along the Hudson as effectively as might be done by any so-called modern optic.

In operation since 1826, Stony Point is the oldest lighthouse on the Hudson.
Ronald J. Foster

STATEN ISLAND LIGHT

Location: New York City
(Staten Island)

Established: 1912

Tower height: 90 feet

Elevation of the focal
plane: 231 feet

Optic: Fresnel (second
order)

Status: Active

Characteristic: Fixed
white

Range: 18 miles

Position: 40° 34' 30
74° 08' 36

Note: Rare British
crystal lens

Below and right courtesy of
Al Pochek

The 90-foot octagonal brick tower rises from high ground that lifts its light more than 230 feet above sea level. Built in 1912, the structure is Edwardian in character. Interestingly, its huge, second-order bivalve lens was imported from England rather than France. Still in use today, the bull's-eye lens produces a fixed white beacon used as a rear-range light. The front-range beacon shines from the West Bank Lighthouse (1901), a cast-iron tower built on a concrete caisson more than 5 miles away.

TO SEE THE LIGHT: Although closed to the public, you can approach the Staten Island tower by way of Lighthouse Avenue, off Richmond Road. The West Bank Lighthouse is located in the open waters of the Lower Hudson Bay. The historic New Dorp Lighthouse (1856), a wooden combination tower and dwelling, is now a private residence. It can be seen from Altmont Street, off Richmond Road. From the Gateway National Recreation Area and Great Kills Park off Hylan Boulevard, you can spot the coffeepot-style Old Orchard Shoal Lighthouse (1893), rising on a caisson about 3 miles to the southeast. Its flashing white and red light remains active.

Bob and Sandra Shanklin, The Lighthouse People

ROBBINS REEF LIGHT

A coffeepot-style, cast-iron tower, the existing Robbins Reef Light replaced an earlier stone structure in 1883. Located on a massive stone pier in the middle of the main channel through the Upper New York Bay, the light remains active, guiding vessels in and out of the great city's busy harbor. The original fourth-order Fresnel lens was replaced by a modern optic when the station was automated in 1966. This offshore light is famous for keeper Kate Walker, who took over the job from her husband when he died in 1885 and faithfully watched the light for the next thirty-three years. Walker handled even the most physically taxing keeper's chores unassisted, and she is credited with saving as many as seventy-five lives.

Although located within sight of the greatest city in the world, the Robbins Reef Lighthouse was nonetheless one of the nations most isolated navigational stations. Walker's children lived with her inside the squat, cylindrical tower, and when fog closed over the station, the mainland must have seemed very distant indeed. When school was in session, Walker rowed her children to Staten Island everyday. She tended the light until 1919, when other keepers replaced her.

TO SEE THE LIGHT: The best way to see this light is from the decks of the Staten Island ferry; www.siferry.com.

Location: New York City (Staten Island)

Established: 1839

Tower height: 45 feet

Elevation of the focal plane: 56 feet

Optic: Modern

Status: Active

Characteristic: Flashes green every 6 seconds

Range: 7 miles

Position: 40° 39' 24 74° 04' 00

Note: Kate Walker served as keeper for 33 years

STATUE OF LIBERTY

Dedicated in 1886 and commissioned as a harbor light that same year, the Statue of Liberty is probably the world's most famous lighthouse. The light in the bronze lady's torch guided ships in and out of the harbor for many years and is still hailed as a guiding light by many landlubbers. The lady herself is 152 feet tall from base to torch; she lifts her lamp a spectacular 305 feet above the ground, making this one of America's loftiest navigational lights. Those who pay homage to Lady Liberty owe much of their deep attachment to her to Emma Lazarus's famous inscription on the pedestal: ". . . give me your tired, your poor, your huddled masses yearning to breathe free . . . send these, the homeless, the tempest-tost to me, I lift my lamp beside the golden door!"

Lady Liberty really is a very big bronze gal, weighing in at 450,000 pounds. Brought to the United States aboard the French frigate *Isere,* she arrived in 214 carefully packed crates, each of them weighing almost a ton. The statue's dimensions lend a better sense of her size: Her right arm is 42 feet long and has a 16-foot-long hand with an index finger almost 8 feet long. Her head is 10 feet thick and her mouth 3 feet wide. Anyone who has ever climbed the statue-not an adventure recommended for the fainthearted-knows that you can actually reach the head, which affords a spectacular view of the New York Harbor. However, for security reasons, the Statue of Liberty's crown and torch are currently off-limits.

TO SEE THE LIGHT: The ferry to Liberty Island and its statue leaves from Battery Park at the lower tip of Manhattan. Passengers can also view the cast-iron, coffeepot-style Robbins Reef Light (1839). Its flashing green light remains in operation. A time pass reservations is required to enter the monument itself. For information, call (266) STATUE4. For further information on the Statue of Liberty National Monument, call (212) 363–3200; for ferry schedules, call (212) 269–5755.

Location: New York City

Established: 1886

Tower height: 303 feet

Status: Deactivated in 1902

Note: Universally recognized symbol of freedom

Bob and Sandra Shanklin, The Lighthouse People

JEFFREY'S HOOK LIGHT

🏠 🚗 🔭 📷

Location: New York City

Established: 1880

Tower height: 40 feet

Elevation of the focal plane: 40 feet

Optic: Modern

Status: Private aid to navigation

Characteristic: Flashes every 3 seconds

Range: 5 miles (estimated)

Position: 40° 31' 01 73° 59' 49

Note: Subject of popular children's story

Perhaps no other port on Earth is so well lit as New York City. A New York-bound navigator could hardly miss the Empire State Building, with its television tower topping out at 1,414 feet. At the harbor entrance the Statue of Liberty, originally intended as a lighthouse, is awash in floodlight. So it is ironic that New York is home to the diminutive Jeffrey's Hook Light, known to many New Yorkers as the "little red lighthouse under the George Washington Bridge."

A steel-plated cylinder only 40 feet tall, the bright red lighthouse is dwarfed by the bridge, which towers hundreds of feet overhead. Built in 1920, the small Jeffrey's Hook tower replaced a pair of simple stake lights, which had stood here since 1889. The lighthouse would serve for less than a dozen years, however, before completion of the George Washington Bridge in 1931 rendered it obsolete. The bridge's massive 3,500-foot span has special lights marking the safe channel for ships moving up and down the Hudson River.

Having lost its job to the bridge, the lighthouse appeared to be headed for oblivion. The Coast Guard intended to dismantle the metal tower and auction it off as scrap. However, the publication of a now-famous children's book, *The Little Red Lighthouse and the Great Gray Bridge*, by Hildegarde Hoyt Swift, stirred up a storm of public protest. The book made the point that, even in a land of giants, "little things and little people" have a vital part to play and must be respected. Faced with a sort of children's crusade to save the lighthouse, the Coast Guard relented and deeded the structure to the New York City Parks

Department. The Jeffrey's Hook Light survives now as a much-loved attraction of New York's Fort Washington Park, and was reactivated in 2002.

TO SEE THE LIGHT: The tower, kept painted bright red by New York City park workers, stands directly under the George Washington Bridge on the Manhattan side of the Hudson. Take the Fort Washington exit off Riverside Drive. For tours call (212) 304–2365.

William G. Kaufhold

STONY POINT LIGHTHOUSE

When its temporary beacon first shined late in the year 1826, the Stony Point Lighthouse became the government's first operational light on the Hudson River. Its final lighting apparatus, installed in 1902, was a fourth-order Fresnel used previously at the Tarrytown Lighthouse. Erected some 20 miles south of West Point, Stony Point's 24-foot structure housed a light that could be seen nearly 22 miles south along the river. Replaced by a skeleton tower in 1925, the original lighthouse now stands high on a promontory in a beautiful state park.

Known as the Stony Point Battlefield State Historic Site, the park commemorates a Revolutionary War assault by Continental infantry on British positions overlooking the Hudson. As an added park attraction, the light has been relit and now shines every night. The fourth-order lens that focuses the beacon is on loan from the U.S. Coast Guard.

TO SEE THE LIGHT: From New York City, take the Palisades Parkway north to exit 15, then follow Routes 106 and 9W through the village of Stony Point to Park Road. The lighthouse is located within the Stony Point Battlefield State Historical Site; call (845) 786–2521.

Location: Stony Point

Established: 1826

Tower height: 30 feet

Elevation of the focal plane: 178 feet

Optic: Fresnel (fourth order)

Status: Deactivated 1925

Characteristic: Flashes every 4 seconds (skeleton tower)

Range: 5 miles

Position: 41° 14' 30
73° 38' 12

Note: Original tower now lit for historical purposes only

RONDOUT CREEK LIGHT

At a wide, sweeping bend in the Hudson River, an old lighthouse marks the harbor entrance of the inland port city of Kingston. The two-story brick dwelling and attached 50-foot-tall tower stand near where the waters of Rondout Creek enter the river.

An earlier lighthouse built at the site in 1880 had to be replaced after a series of dikes shifted the entrance well away from the original shoreline. The existing structure, known locally as Rondout Two, was completed in 1915 and has remained in service ever since. Nearly surrounded by the waters of the Hudson and Rondout Creek, it stands on a solid concrete pier.

The Coast Guard automated the light in 1954 and in recent years replaced the original fifth-order Fresnel lens with a modern plastic device. The dwelling stood empty for more than thirty years before being leased to the Hudson River Maritime Center for eventual use as a museum. With assistance from the City of Kingston, the interior of the dwelling has been refurbished and filled with historic exhibits, including a display on the lives of keepers and their families. The museum is open on weekends during the summer and fall.

TO SEE THE LIGHT: Reach Kingston via I–87 (New York Thruway) or Route 9. For museum hours contact the Hudson River Maritime Center at (845) 338–0071. Downriver a few miles from Kingston is the Esopus Meadows Lighthouse (1879), now undergoing restoration by local preservationists. Located in mid-channel, it cannot be reached from land but can be seen from points along Route 9 on the east side of the river.

Location: Kingston

Established: 1880

Tower height: 48 feet

Elevation of the focal plane: 52 feet

Optic: Modern

Status: Active

Characteristic: Flashes every 6 seconds

Range: 9 miles

Position: 41° 55' 16
73° 57' 44

Note: Offshore river light

William G. Kaufhold

SAUGERTIES LIGHT

Location: Saugerties

Established: 1836

Tower height: 42 feet

Elevation of the focal
plane: 46 feet

Optic: Modern

Status: Active

Characteristic: Occults
every 4 seconds

Range: 5 miles

Position: 42° 04' 18
73° 55' 48

Note: Beacon dark from
1954 until 1990

A stone lighthouse stood beside the Hudson River at Saugerties as early as 1836, but after about thirty years, time and flood-waters had damaged it beyond repair. In the late 1860s construction began on a new Saugerties lighthouse, which went into service in 1869. The two-story brick dwelling and attached tower were built on a low stone caisson only a few feet above high water (the Hudson has tides of up to 4 feet). The octagonal iron lantern atop the square tower contained a sixth-order—the smallest available—Fresnel lens.

Located at the confluence of Esopus Creek and the Hudson River, the Saugerties Lighthouse guided several generations of river pilots. It was finally closed in 1954, bringing to an end eighty-five years of continuous service. Afterward the Coast Guard established a new, automated light on a nearby steel tower.

Abandoned for more than twenty years, the old lighthouse fell into a sad state of disrepair and seemed on the verge of collapse.

A group of concerned local citizens then formed the Saugerties Lighthouse Conservancy and set about raising money to restore the dilapidated structure. Many years of prodigious conservancy efforts have led to a handsome restoration, and the lighthouse is now open to the public as a museum.

TO SEE THE LIGHT: Handsomely restored by the Saugerties Lighthouse Conservancy, the lighthouse is now a museum open to the public on weekends. The conservancy now works to preserve other lighthouses. You may contact the organization at (845) 247–0656.

Ronald J. Foster

HUDSON CITY LIGHT

It's a rare thing for a major navigational light to shine more than 100 miles from the nearest expanse of open water. This can be said, however, of the Hudson City Light. In fact, not one but two mountain ranges, the Catskills and Berkshires, stand between this light and the sea. Established in 1874 to mark the dangerous Middle Ground Flats near the inland port cities of Hudson and Athens, New York, the Hudson City Light still guides ships to this day. The flats have scarred or breached the hulls of more than one river freighter and barge.

The brick dwelling and 48-foot tower stand on a limestone pier that protects the structure from ice floes. The tower is topped by a small, octagonal lantern room, which once held a fifth-order Fresnel lens. Today the light is automated, and the building is maintained by a local conservation organization dedicated to preserving the old light.

While winter ice was always a threat to lighthouses and other structures along the river, it also provided seasonal employment for many hard-working laborers along this stretch of the Hudson. The thick, clear river ice was sawed into enormous blocks and stored in insulated warehouses for sale during warm-weather months. During the late nineteenth and early twentieth centuries, this Hudson River bounty kept iceboxes cold and rattled in the drink glasses of sweltering city dwellers every summer.

TO SEE THE LIGHT: Hudson City can be reached from New York City or Albany via I–87 or Route 9. The lighthouse itself stands well out in the Hudson River and can be reached only by boat. Contact the Hudson-Athens Lighthouse Perservaton Society for tour information; (518) 828–5294.

U.S. Coast Guard

Location: Hudson City, New York

Established: 1874

Tower height: 48 feet

Elevation of the focal plane: 52 feet

Optic: Modern

Status: Active

Characteristic: Flashes every 2.5 seconds

Range: 6 miles

Position: 41° 52' 07
73° 56' 29

Note: Inland light more than 100 miles from the Atlantic

CHAPTER THREE
THE GREAT LAKES: ROCK ISLAND TO BARCELONA

Precisely because of their status as navigational markers, light-houses are closely identified with certain geographic or natural features, for instance, Long Island, the Hudson River, or the Great Lakes. In North America one such feature stands out from all the others: Niagara Falls.

Actually a pair of falls, the American and Horseshoe, one on either side of the United States–Canadian border, they form what is arguably the world's most popular and most visited natural wonder. More than forty million gallons of water plunge over them every minute. This unforgettable display of nature's raw power has inspired poets, politicians, and artists, not to mention generations of couples who have flocked to the falls to celebrate their marriages.

The falls also bring about a marriage of continental waters. At Niagara, a hard-rock plug of immense proportion serves as a natural dam which impounds the largest body of freshwater in the world. Behind the falls are Lakes Erie, Huron, Michigan, and Superior. To the east is Lake Ontario, and together with the St. Lawrence River, the five lakes serve as a 1000-mile-long liquid highway linking the Atlantic Ocean with the North American heartland.

For hundreds of years, the lakes have been used to move the abundant resources and produce of the Midwest to markets in the East. The commerce generated by the lakes has contributed greatly to the prosperity of the United States and Canada, but a high price has been paid for it. Their waters frequently tossed by towering, storm-driven waves, the lakes are far from placid, and their low and often featureless shores are lined with dangerous shoals and shallows. Thousands of freighters and other large ships have been lost in the lakes and along the St. Lawrence.

To make navigation safer, a sparkling chain of lights were established to guide mariners from the mouth of the river all the way to Duluth at the far end of Lake Superior. Many of the finest and most historic of these navigational lights can be found in New York, along the shores of Lakes Ontario and Erie. Some date back to the early 1800s, when the nation was still young. The first light at Fort Niagara was shone as far back as 1782, before the end of the Revolutionary War.

RESTORATION OF THE BUFFALO LIGHT-
HOUSE WAS UNDERTAKEN IN 1987 BY
THE BUFFALO LIGHTHOUSE ASSOCIATION,
INC. WITH THE ASSISTANCE OF THE
UNITED STATES COAST GUARD.

BUFFALO LIGHTHOUSE ASSOCIATION
BOARD OF DIRECTORS

MICHAEL N. VOGEL
RICHARD PETRI
JAMES J. RZAD
STASIA Z. VOGEL ESQ.
NANCY F. SMITH
CAPT. ROBERT C. HOULE USCG
DAVID K. MAC LEOD
THOMAS R. JOHNSTON
CMDR. STEVEN CORNELL, USCG
BARBARA BIELECKI
JAMES T. CLAUSS

MAJOR SUPPORT FOR THE LIGHTHOUSE
RESTORATION WAS PROVIDED BY
THE JUNIOR LEAGUE OF BUFFALO

AND BY

THE BUFFALO SESQUICENTENNIAL COMMITTEE
THE MARGARET L. WENDT FOUNDATION
THE BUFFALO FOUNDATION
THE CAMERON BAIRD FOUNDATION
THE UNITED STATES COAST GUARD FOUNDATION
THE BUFFALO NEWS
MERCHANTS INSURANCE GROUP
THE NEW YORK STATE COUNCIL ON THE ARTS
COMPASS LEASING INC.
LIGHTHOUSE PROPERTIES LTD.
NICHOLSON & HALL
MICHAEL R. MADIA
K & E FABRICATING CO. INC.
AMERICAN STEAMSHIP CO.
MR. & MRS. BURT P. FLICKINGER JR.
ARVIN/CALSPAN CORP.
RUPP RENTAL & SALES CORP.
RICHARD W. DESBECKER
ARMY NATIONAL GUARD 152d ENGINEER BN, NY
RICHARD PETRI

This Buffalo Lighthouse tower was built in 1833 to shed light on Lake Erie.

OGDENSBURG HARBOR LIGHTHOUSE

Location: Ogdensburg

Established: 1834

Tower height: 65 feet

Status: Deactivated

Note: Now a private residence

Located on the St. Lawrence River a few dozen miles from Lake Ontario, the town of Ogdensburg has been recognized by many as the gateway to the Great Lakes. Because of the strategic importance of this place, the French built a fort here in 1749. Founded by the famous French missionary Abbé François Picquet, Fort La Presentation served as a mission, trading center, and school as well as a key military outpost. The fort was burned and abandoned by its French defenders as British troops closed in during the final months of the French and Indian War.

On the ruins of La Presentation, the British built Fort Oswegatchie, which helped them control access to the Great Lakes during the Revolutionary War. Following the war, American troops under Colonel Samuel Ogden took possession of the fort. The thriving settlement that grew up here was later named for Ogden, and eventually, Ogdensburg became a vital St. Lawrence River port.

In 1834 a lighthouse was built on the site of the original French fort. The Ogdensburg Harbor Lighthouse was given a 65-foot limestone tower and spacious attached dwelling. Refurbished in 1900, the lighthouse still stands today. The light itself has been inactive for many years, and the keeper's dwelling is now used as a private residence.

TO SEE THE LIGHT: Now on private property, the old lighthouse is off limits to the public and can only be viewed from the water.

ROCK ISLAND LIGHTHOUSE

📖 📷

Location: Rock Island

Established: 1847

Tower height: 68 feet

Status: Deactivated 1958

Note: Guards an island in the St. Lawrence River

To reach the Great Lakes from the Atlantic Ocean, ships must push several hundred miles up the ever-narrowing St. Lawrence River. Toward the end of this river journey are the Thousand Islands, which guard the approaches to Lake Ontario. Six lighthouses were built along the river and among the islands to guide ships and warn them of obstacles. One of the best preserved of these is the Rock Island Lighthouse, established in 1847 and rebuilt in 1882.

The Rock Island Lighthouse has its feet in the river. Built just off the island on a concrete foundation, the 60-foot, conical limestone tower is connected to land by a stone walkway. The lantern once held a sixth-order Fresnel lens, but during the 1950s, the station was deactivated and the old lens removed. At one time the lamps were powered by a gasoline generator located in a separate structure near the dwelling. Active for almost a century, the light served countless vessels steaming along the St. Lawrence, going to and from the Great Lakes.

TO SEE THE LIGHT: Rock Island is accessible only from the water, and while no public transportation to the island is available, private boats

may stop here. The lighthouse is usually open to the public from 8:00 A.M. to 4:30 P.M. during the summer months, but it is best to make sure by calling ahead. For information write the Great Lakes Seaway Trail, P.O. Box 660, Sackets Harbor, NY 13685, or call (800) 732–9298. The lighthouse can also be seen from Thousand Island Park, on Wellesley Island, and from the community of Fisher's Landing, off Route 12 at Route 180,

Bob and Sandra Shanklin, The Lighthouse People

just a few miles southwest of the Thousand Island Bridge. For information on events and facilities in the Thousand Islands region, write the Thousand Islands International Council, 43373 Collins Landing, Alexandria Bay, NY 13607, or call (800) 8–ISLAND.

The Fresnel Lens in America

Invented in 1822 by French physicist Augustin Fresnel, these big prismatic glass lenses were designed to snatch every flicker of light from even the smallest lamp and concentrate it into a powerful beam that could be seen from dozens of miles away. Fresnel's elegant lenses did their job so well they soon became standard equipment in lighthouses throughout much of the world.

However, the new technology was virtually ignored for several decades in the United States, where Winslow Lewis's far less effective parabolic reflectors were employed right up until the middle of the nineteenth century. One reason for this was the considerable expense of the highly polished lenses, which had to be imported from France.

Another was the bureaucratic fussiness of Stephen Pleasonton, the U.S. Treasury auditor who served for many years as head of the nation's lighthouse system. Displaying undisguised favoritism for Lewis, a personal friend, Pleasonton continued to equip U.S. lighthouses with his outdated reflectors.

The third-order Fresnel at Dunkirk Light has been operating since 1857.

In 1852, stewardship of America's navigational lights passed to a Lighthouse Board consisting of military officers, engineers, harbor masters, and experienced seamen. The board immediately undertook a complete overhaul of America's lighthouses. As part of this effort, most lighthouses were fitted with sparkling new Fresnel lenses. Some of these lenses, installed during the years before the Civil War, remain in service to this day.

Fresnel lenses are as effective and useful today as they were 150 years ago. Unlike so many other technologies, this one reached its peak of sophistication very early in the Industrial Revolution.

TIBBETTS POINT LIGHT

Lighthouses are nearly always strategically located, but that is especially true of Tibbetts Point Light in Cape Vincent, New York. Its light marks the entrance to the St. Lawrence River and the beginning of the last leg of any journey from the Great Lakes to the Atlantic. Recognizing the importance of the place to commercial shipping, the government placed a light station here in 1827. The stone tower stood 59 feet high and employed a whale-oil lamp and reflector lighting system.

The light tower that can be seen at Cape Vincent today replaced the earlier lighthouse in 1854. Its 69-foot stucco tower was given a fourth-order Fresnel lens lit by a fifty-candle-power oil lamp. A steam-powered fog signal began operation in 1896. The station was automated by the Coast Guard in 1981.

Cape Vincent has spectacular sunsets, and the light grounds offer an excellent place to view and photograph them. Nearby are several historic islands, including Wolfe Island, named for the British general who captured Quebec, and Carleton Island, a frequent gathering place for large Mohawk war parties.

Location: Cape Vincent

Established: 1827

Tower height: 59 feet

Elevation of the focal plane: 69 feet

Optic: Fresnel (fourth order)

Status: Active

Characteristic: Occults every 10 seconds

Range: 16 miles

Position: 44° 06' 00
76° 22' 12

Note: Marks the eastern end of Lake Ontario

TO SEE THE LIGHT: From Watertown follow Highway 12F and then Highway 12E to Cape Vincent. Turn left onto Broadway and drive 2.5 miles to the light. The grounds and museum (315–654–2700) are open daily, whereas the youth hostel located in the caretaker's house operates mid-May to mid-October. For hostel reservations call (315) 654–3450. To the southwest, near Sackets Harbor, is the 73-foot tower of the Stony Point Lighthouse (1837). From New York Route 3, follow Military Road and then Lighthouse Road to Stony Point.

Jim Crowley

EAST CHARITY SHOAL LIGHT

Few waterways are more strategic than the St. Lawrence River, which opens the heart of North America to shipping from the Atlantic. The waters off Tibbetts Point, New York, at the eastern end of Lake Ontario, serve as the portal for freighters and other vessels entering and exiting the river. Navigating this heavily trafficked maritime highway is always difficult, and pilots must take special care to avoid East Charity Shoal, a dangerous obstacle located about 6 miles from shore.

For more than seventy years, a lighthouse has warned mariners away from the shoal. Marked on navigational charts as the East Charity Shoal Light, it stands on a stone and cement crib built in open water directly over the shoal. Atop the crib a 30-foot octagonal tower rests on a 10-foot-high concrete pedestal. The massive crib and pedestal protect the cast-iron tower from ice and storm-driven waves.

Although the light here was established in 1935, the East Charity Shoal tower has the appearance of a much older structure—and it is. The tower was built in 1877 at Vermilion, Ohio, where it served for more than sixty years. Then, during the winter of 1929, a bulldozer-like crush of lake ice nearly bowled it over. The severely damaged iron tower was taken to Buffalo, New York, for repairs, and a few years later was moved to East Charity Shoal, where it can still be seen today.

TO SEE THE LIGHT: Since it is located several miles from shore, the only way to get a close-up view of the lighthouse is from the water.

Location: off Tibbetts Point

Established: 1935

Tower height: 52 feet feet

Elevation of the focal plane: 52 feet

Optic: Modern

Status: Active

Characteristic: Flashes every 4 seconds

Range: 9 miles

Position: 44° 02' 12 76° 28' 34

Note: Tower moved here from Vermilion, Ohio

SELKIRK LIGHT (POINT ONTARIO)

Although its beacon served lake sailors for little more than twenty years, the Selkirk Light is one of the more fascinating and historic buildings on the Great Lakes. Built in 1838, it was taken out of service in 1859, when the local fishing and shipbuilding industries began to fade. Fortunately, the old lighthouse has survived. Its gabled fieldstone dwelling and old-style lantern are of considerable architectural and historical interest.

The first settlers came to Port Ontario to harvest the Atlantic salmon that arrived here in prodigious numbers to spawn. The fishermen were followed by sailors and shipbuilders, who built homes beside the lake and along the banks of the appropriately named Salmon River. In one way or another, most of the men in the area relied for their living on Lake Ontario. With its dangerous, unpredictable weather, the lake was a fickle and sometimes death-dealing friend. That is why, according to legend, houses hereabouts have an unusually large number of windows, for the wives of fishermen and sailors kept a constant eye on the lake for some sign of their menfolks.

Built for $3,000 by local contractors from stone quarried nearby, the old dwelling is one of a kind. The small lantern room projecting through the roof is also highly unusual. It is of an early type in use before Fresnel lenses became common (about the middle of the nineteenth century). Originally, the lantern held a 14-inch parabolic reflector and eight mineral-oil lamps. The light could be seen from about 14 miles out on the lake. Shortly before it was discontinued, the outdated reflector system was replaced by a sixth-order Fresnel lens.

When the Salmon River began to silt up and ship traffic dropped off, the government saw little need for a light here. The building was eventually sold for use as a private residence and then as a hotel. Although its lantern was dark for more than 130 years, the old lighthouse is now back in operation. In 1989 the owners received permission from the Coast Guard to place an automated light in the lantern. The light is designated a Class 11 navigational aid.

TO SEE THE LIGHT: Take Route 3 to Port Ontario; then follow Lake Road to its end. The light stands near the mouth of the Salmon River. Contact Selkirk Lighthouse, 6 Lake Road Extension, P.O. Box 228, Pulaski, NY 13142; (315) 298–6688. Overnight stays in the lighthouse are available.

Location: Pulaski

Established: 1838

Tower height: 32 feet

Elevation of the focal plane: 49 feet

Optic: Modern

Status: Private aid to navigation

Characteristic: Flashes every 2 seconds

Range: 14 miles

Position: 43° 34' 24
76° 12' 06

Note: Dark for 130 years, light was restored in 1989

🖺 📷

Location: Oswego

Established: 1822

Tower height: 57 feet

Elevation of the focal
plane: 57 feet

Optic: Fresnel
(fourth order)

Status: Active

Characteristic: Alternates
white and red every 5
seconds

Range: 15 miles

Position: 43° 28' 24
76° 31' 00

Note: Sole survivor of
four Oswego lighthouses

OSWEGO WEST PIERHEAD LIGHT

O ver the course of almost two centuries, several different light-houses have served the port city of Oswego, guiding vessels into and out of its bustling harbor. The first, a simple stone tower and keeper's dwelling built in 1822, stood at Fort Ontario on the east bank of the Oswego River.

As shipping on Lake Ontario increased and Oswego grew into an important commercial center, the need for a better, more power-ful light became apparent. In 1836 a fine new lighthouse was built, at the end of a long pier on the west side of the harbor. An octago-nal gray tower with attached oil room, it boasted a third-order Fresnel lens displaying a fixed white light that could be seen from 15 miles out on the lake.

Tended by several generations of keepers, the light burned for almost a century. The hearts of Ontario's sailors and Oswego's old-timers were saddened when the wrecking crews pulled down the old tower in 1930.

The government had no intention of leaving Oswego's harbor unmarked for long, however, and plans were already in the making for a third lighthouse. By 1934 it was in service. Consisting of a rel-atively short metal tower and a small attached dwelling, each with white walls and a red roof, the lighthouse stands on a concrete pier at the end of a long stone breakwater. Fitted with a rotating, fourth-order Fresnel lens, the lantern displays a flashing red light. Tinted window panels in the lantern give the light its characteristic color.

In 1942 several coastguardsmen drowned only a short dis-tance from the lighthouse, during what was to have been a routine exchange of keepers. Not long afterward Coast Guard officials decided to automate the light.

Another historic Oswego attraction is Fort Ontario. Built as a frontier bastion by the British in 1755, during the French and Indian War, Fort Ontario fell to the forces of the Marquis de Montcalm in 1756. The French destroyed the fort before retreating toward Quebec, where they were eventually defeated. The British rebuilt the fortress, only to see it overrun by an army of American revolutionaries in 1778. During the War of 1812, the British returned to bombard and overwhelm the fort. The undermanned defenders had only six cannons, which were in such bad shape that they had been con-demned. Fort Ontario also saw service in the Civil War and in World War II, when it was used as a refugee center.

TO SEE THE LIGHT: The public is not allowed to visit the light, but its white walls and red roof are visible from several places in Oswego, including Bretbeck Park. To reach the park from Route 104, turn toward the lake on West First Street, then left onto Van Buren, then right onto Lake Street. The park is just beyond Wright's Landing. While in the area, take time to visit historic Fort Ontario, where the keeper's residence of the original 1822 lighthouse can still be seen.

SODUS POINT LIGHT

Location: Sodus Point

Established: 1825

Tower height: 49 feet
(outer)

Elevation of the focal
plane: 51 feet (outer)

Optic: Modern

Status: Active (outer)

Characteristic: Interrupted
every 6 seconds

Range: 10 miles

Position: 43° 16' 36
76° 58' 30

Note: Historic stone lighthouse on shore serves as
a museum

The Old Sodus Lighthouse
(below) was replaced by
the currently active pier
light (opposite).

On June 19, 1813, the citizens of sleepy Sodus Point, New York, had an uncharacteristically noisy day. A British fleet had sailed across Lake Ontario and rudely awakened them with cannon fire. The British fleet landed troops, but the redcoats were stopped and eventually driven off by a hastily gathered force of militia. To raise the alarm, a local horseman rode, Paul Revere-style, through the country-side to warn farmers and villagers that "the British are coming."

From 1825 until just after the turn of the twentieth century, Sodus Point Lighthouse offered mariners a different sort of warning: Its bright beacon announced clearly that land was near. Unexpected encounters with land are nearly always fatal to ships and all too often to their crews as well. Ships' captains and residents in this area had petitioned Congress for a light to guide sailors safely into Sodus Bay. Eventually, they were rewarded by construction of a rough split-stone tower and dwelling.

Completed during the administration of President John Quincy Adams, these structures remained in use for more than forty years. Following the Civil War they fell into a sad state of disrepair, and the government replaced them with a 45-foot-high, square stone tower and attached two-story dwelling. The light has been inactive since 1901, its job taken over by the nearby pier light. Today the station structures are maintained by the Sodus Bay Historical Society. The dwelling now contains a delightful maritime museum. Visitors will want to see the 3.5-order Fresnel lens in the tower.

TO SEE THE LIGHT: Take Route 104, then Route 14 north to the village of Sodus Point and turn left onto Ontario Street (at the fire hall). The Old Sodus Lighthouse is open weekends, July to mid-October. For hours call (315) 483–4936.

CHARLOTTE–GENESEE LIGHTHOUSE

📠 🚪 🗒 📷

Location: Rochester

Established: 1822

Tower height: 40 feet

Status: Deactivated 1884

Note: Second oldest lighthouse on the Great Lakes

Completed in 1822 at a cost of $3,301 and dropped from active service in 1884, the Charlotte–Genesee Lighthouse is now the second-oldest lighthouse on the Great Lakes. The grand old lighthouse owes its continued existence in part to students of nearby Charlotte High School, who have made it their symbol. In 1965, when it was rumored that the lighthouse would be torn down, students at the school began a successful campaign to save the structure. Responding to student petitions and other public pressure, the government handed the lighthouse over to the Charlotte–Genesee Lighthouse Historical Society. The station has now been restored, and its museum is operated under a permanent charter from New York State. The Coast Guard contributed a Fresnel lens from its Cleveland, Ohio, station to the restoration effort.

More than 170 years ago, the 40-foot-high, octagonal limestone tower was erected on the edge of a bluff overlooking the mouth of the Genesee River and Lake Ontario beyond. David Denman, the station's first keeper, lived beside the tower in a rustic, two-room limestone cottage. Each night Denman trudged up the tower steps to light the ten Argand lamps that produced the light concentrated by a set of reflectors. These relatively inefficient reflectors were exchanged for a fourth-order Fresnel lens in 1852. The current two-and-a-half-story brick dwelling replaced the cottage in 1863.

The antique Lens at Charlotte–Genesee Lighthouse.

As part of renovations at the Genesee light station, government crews built a pier, placing a second small lighthouse tower at the end. In 1853 an August nor'easter sent waves crashing over the pier, making it extremely difficult for keeper Samuel Phillips to reach the tower on the pier and fire up the lamp there. Former lighthouse keeper Cuyler Cook happened to be nearby with a boat and offered to row Phillips out to the tower. Cook paid for this generosity with his life. While Phillips was tending the lamp, the waves swamped Cook's boat and drowned him.

In 1884 lighthouse officials decided to move the primary light station's apparatus to the pier and abandon the original lighthouse. Luckily, the old octagonal tower survived more than a century of disuse and remains today as a reminder of an earlier, more romantic era. In 1974 the Genesee Lighthouse was placed on the National Register of Historic Places.

TO SEE THE LIGHT: In Rochester take Seaway Trail (Lakeshore Boulevard); then follow Lake Avenue north to Holy Cross Church, or take the Lake Ontario State Parkway to Lake Avenue. The lighthouse parking lot is behind the church. Grounds are open daily, and the Charlotte–Genesee Lighthouse Historical Society opens the tower and dwelling to the public on weekends. Write to Charlotte–Genesee Lighthouse Museum, 70 Lighthouse Street, Rochester, NY 14612 or call (585) 621–6179. To the west of Rochester near the Lake Ontario State Parkway is the site of the Braddock Point Lighthouse (1890s). Much of the tower is gone, and the Victorian-style dwelling is now a private residence. What remains of the old station is best viewed from the water off the point.

THIRTY MILE POINT LIGHT

Location: Somerset

Established: 1876

Tower height: 61 feet

Elevation of the focal plane: 71 feet

Optic: Modern

Status: Private aid to navigation

Characteristic: Flashes every 10 seconds

Range: 10 miles (estimated)

Position: 43° 22' 30
78° 29' 11

Note: Reactivated in 1998 after 39 years of inactivity

S ome say that Golden Hill takes its name from the glittering army payroll supposedly washed or brought ashore from the wreck of the British fighting ship HMS *Ontario*. There have been more than a few unsuccessful attempts to dig up the treasure. A less dramatic explanation for the name, which has the support of local historians, is the profusion of goldenrod that once bloomed on an island off the point. The island has been eroded away, along with the dangerous sandbar that once lay off the point. Yet rumors of buried treasure at Golden Hill persist.

As long ago as 1834, a local farmer told his neighbors of being startled by a group of men who had rowed up Golden Hill Creek to dig up a chest from the creek bank. He said that they took the chest back to a waiting schooner. Similar stories were told during the Prohibition era of the twentieth century. It is said that smugglers often brought illicit shipments of liquor ashore here.

The Thirty Mile Point Lighthouse was built on Golden Hill in 1876, at a cost of $90,000. It remained in service until 1959, when the light was automated and transferred to a slender steel tower nearby. The gray square-cut stones of the original tower were shipped from Chaumont Bay near the St. Lawrence River and then hauled up the steep banks of Golden Hill.

A Fresnel lens manufactured in France was installed in the 8-foot-diameter lantern room. The handmade French lens concentrated the light produced by a kerosene flame to a strength of 600,000 candlepower. Sailors could see the light from up to 18 miles away. In 1885 the kerosene flame was replaced with one of the earliest electric bulbs ever placed in a lighthouse. The light, produced by the combination of the old Fresnel lens and Mr. Thomas Edison's newfangled invention, became the strongest on Lake Ontario and the fourth strongest on the Great Lakes.

TO SEE THE LIGHT: To reach Golden Hill State Park, take Route 18 to Route 269 north; then turn west on Lower Lake Road. The park offers campsites, picnic tables, a marina, and an engaging nature trail in addition to the self-guided lighthouse tour. Call (716) 795–3885.

Around 1781 the British built a stone light tower atop Fort Niagara, which they had captured in 1759, near the end of the French and Indian War. The fort was a natural place for a navigational light, as it overlooked the strategic juncture of the Niagara River and Lake Ontario and marked the site of overland portages around Niagara Falls. Following the American Revolution, the U.S. Army took possession of the fort, but by 1796 had stopped using the lighthouse.

In 1823 a light once again shone from Fort Niagara, this time from a wooden tower. The light did not signal a revival of the old fort's commercial significance, however, for within two years the Erie Canal began diverting most of the river's east-west traffic away from the old Niagara Portage. When Canada opened its Welland Canal in 1829, Buffalo, on Lake Erie, became a booming commercial center overnight, whereas Fort Niagara settled into the life of a minor trading port.

In 1872 a new 50-foot octagonal stone tower was completed on the lake shoreline just south of the fort, and the signal at Fort Niagara was extinguished. This new tower had 11 feet added to its height in 1900, enabling its beacon to shine out some 25 miles over Lake Ontario. The refurbished tower included a watch room, complete with a built-in desk for the keeper. A lamp-oil shed sat at the tower's base. Deactivated in 1993, the lighthouse is one of many exhibits in Old Fort Niagara State Park, where it placidly watches over the park's numerous military reenactments. Although dark now, the station's old fourth-order Fresnel lens remains in place. Mariners on Lake Ontario may still rely on a modern beacon shining from a strictly utilitarian light tower placed here by the Coast Guard.

TO SEE THE LIGHT: From Niagara, New York, take the Robert Moses Parkway to the Old Fort Niagara State Park entrance. Once inside the park, follow signs to the lighthouse. Visitors should set aside plenty of time to enjoy this historic site, which is a gold mine for history buffs. Living-history exhibits and military reenactments are part of the park's summer offerings. The fort is open daily throughout the year. Call Old Fort Niagara at (716) 745-7611.

Location: Youngstown

Established: 1781

Tower height: 61 feet

Elevation of the focal plane: 91 feet

Optic: Modern (existing beacon)

Status: Deactivated 1993

Characteristic: Occults every 4 seconds (existing beacon)

Range: 15 miles (existing beacon)

Position: 43° 15' 42 79° 03' 48

Note: On the grounds of a historic fort

The French Castle

In 1759 the British captured Fort Niagara, which had come to be known as the "French Castle," and was one of the most valued prizes of the French and Indian War. Only fifteen years after their victory over the French, the British found themselves once more at war in America. This time the fight was against their own unruly colonists. During the Revolutionary War, the British maintained a powerful navy on the Great Lakes. Among their most formidable lake warships was HMS *Ontario*. Launched during the late spring of 1780, she was at least 80 feet long and square rigged like an oceangoing fighting ship. Armed with sixteen 6-pound cannons and six 4-pounders, she had more than enough firepower to crush any American vessel that might challenge her mastery of Lake Ontario. The weather and the lake itself, however, could not be fought with cannon shot and gunpowder. The *Ontario* was destined to lose her only battle—with one of the Great Lake's notorious autumn storms.

Late in October 1780 the *Ontario* weighed anchor and set sail from Niagara, bound for Oswego, New York, with a load of British soldiers, military supplies, and an army payroll chest brimming with gold and silver coins. On Halloween a gale came whistling out of the west, and by the time it had blown itself out the following morning, the *Ontario* was gone. Vanishing along with her were four women, five children, several Indians, and more than seventy soldiers and seamen. Settlers found dozens of British army caps bobbing in the waves along the south shore of the lake; but there were no other clues to the fate of the ship or its passengers, crew, and cargo. Treasure hunters, interested in valuable relics—not to mention the payroll chest—have searched endlessly for the wreck. Most believe the *Ontario* met her end near Thirty Mile Point. The discovery in 1954 of a very old anchor not far from the point lends weight to this opinion, but the ship herself has never been found.

Ironically, countless sailors may owe their lives indirectly to the sinking of the *Ontario*. The loss of this fine ship alerted British

authorities to the need for better navigation markers on the Great Lakes. In 1781, the year after the *Ontario* disaster, they placed a light, fueled by whale oil, on the roof of Fort Niagara, at the mouth of the Niagara River. The French had built the old stone fortress in 1726 to help protect fur traders portaging their pelts from the upper lakes. The fort and its light, the first established on the Great Lakes, became the property of the United States following the Revolutionary War. Within a few years after the newly independent United States of America occupied Fort Niagara, however, the fortress lighthouse was discontinued. The tower atop the fort is shown in drawings of the structure as late as 1803, but by 1806 it was gone.

Not until 1823 did another beacon, with a wooden tower, go into service atop the old French Castle.

The Light at Fort Niagara once shown from atop an old French fortress.

BUFFALO MAIN LIGHTHOUSE

I n 1805 the U.S. government designated the then-Village of Buffalo a port of entry and made plans to build a lighthouse there. Political squabbling delayed construction, and when British troops burned Buffalo during the War of 1812, it began to look as if the lighthouse might never be built. Buffalo recovered, however, and in 1818 the tower was finally completed.

With the opening of the Erie Canal in 1825, Buffalo became one of the fastest growing cities in America and its port one of the busiest in the world. In 1833 a new octagonal limestone tower signaled Buffalo's growing importance as a commercial center. This tower stood at the end of a 1,400-foot-long pier, its beam shining lakeward from a lantern some 68 feet above the lake.

A new breakwater station went up in 1872. Built at the far end of a 4,000-foot-long breakwater, the tower boasted a fourth-order fixed red light. The old 1833 tower stood empty and neglected for many years, but during the early 1960s, citizens began raising money to restore it. In 1987 the beacon was temporarily relit to help celebrate Buffalo's first International Friendship Festival.

TO SEE THE LIGHT: The Buffalo Main Lighthouse is on the grounds of a Coast Guard station; however, since 1985 it has been leased to the Buffalo Lighthouse Association. Nearby is the rather extraordinary Buffalo Bottle Light (early 1900s), which looks like a cross between a buoy and light tower. Take I–190 to the Church Street exit; then turn right at the first traffic signal onto Lower Terrace. Follow signs to the Erie Basin Marina and Buffalo Main Lighthouse. The lighthouse is best viewed, however, from the Naval and Serviceman's Park, across the river in downtown Buffalo.

Location: Buffalo

Established: 1818

Tower height: 61 feet

Elevation of the focal plane: 75 feet

Status: Deactivated 1914

Note: Revered Buffalo landmark

DUNKIRK (POINT GRATIOT) LIGHT

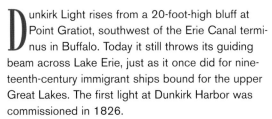

Dunkirk Light rises from a 20-foot-high bluff at Point Gratiot, southwest of the Erie Canal terminus in Buffalo. Today it still throws its guiding beam across Lake Erie, just as it once did for nineteenth-century immigrant ships bound for the upper Great Lakes. The first light at Dunkirk Harbor was commissioned in 1826.

The first lighthouse at Point Gratiot, which became popularly known as Lighthouse Point, was completed in 1827 by Buffalo contractor Jesse Peck. It stood a short distance from the current 62-foot-high tower, which replaced it in 1875.

Early attempts were made here to substitute natural gas for the whale oil typically used to fuel lighthouse lamps. These experiments were not successful, however. In 1857 the lantern was fitted with a third-order Fresnel lens, which produced a 15,000-candle-power flash every ninety seconds. The light could be seen from 17 miles offshore. Today the light station at Point Gratiot serves as a military memorial as well as a lighthouse museum. Point Gratiot is believed to be named for Charles Gratiot, the same U.S. Army engineer for whom Fort Gratiot, on Michigan's St. Clair River, is named.

TO SEE THE LIGHT: The lighthouse complex is in Dunkirk, just off Route 5, which parallels the lakeshore northwest of the New York State Thruway. The complex is open daily from April through November and at other times upon request. Call ahead to find out about special events such as War of 1812 reenactments, craft shows, and lighthouse moonlight cruises; (716) 366–5050.

Location: Point Gratiot

Established: 1829

Tower height: 62 feet

Elevation of the focal plane: 82 feet

Optic: Fresnel (third order)

Status: Active

Characteristic: Occults every 4 seconds

Range: 16 miles

Position: 42° 29' 36
79° 21' 12

Note: Keeper's house now a museum

Disasters at Dunkirk

The first light at Dunkirk Harbor was commissioned in 1826, only a few years after one of the earliest recorded disasters on eastern Lake Erie; one of many.

Launched in 1818 at Black Rock, New York, the paddle wheeler *Walk-in-the-Water* was the lake's first steamboat. But the power of steam could not altogether overcome the forces of nature, and in October 1818 this famous steamboat foundered on a sandbar in heavy weather.

The 132-foot-long, 32-foot-beam *Walk-in-the-Water* was en route from Buffalo to Detroit with a load of passengers and freight. Passage on the one-and-a-half-day cruise was $18.00 for a cabin and $7.00 for steerage. This particular trip turned out not to be such a bargain; though luckily, all the passengers were saved. Even the ship's huge steam engine was salvaged.

In 1841 the *Erie,* bound from Buffalo to Chicago, burned, with the loss of 141 lives, just three miles east of Dunkirk. The tragedy was blamed on painters who had placed buckets of turpentine and varnish on the deck immediately above the *Erie*'s boilers. In addition to her crew of thirty, the *Erie* carried 140 German and Swiss immigrants. The steamboat *De Witt Clinton,* which had just left Dunkirk, rescued twenty-seven survivors.

On October 14, 1893, the wooden steamboat *Dean Richmond,* named for a railway builder, foundered in heavy weather near Dunkirk. Built in Cleveland in 1864, the *Dean Richmond* made regular runs between Buffalo and Chicago. She left her last port of call—Toledo, Ohio—on October 13, 1893, with a cargo of bagged meal and flour, copper sheets, $50,000 worth of pig zinc, and $141,000 in gold and silver bullion. Gale-force winds battered her as she steamed eastward, and the unsecured copper sheets stowed on deck began to shift. The *Richmond* is believed to have tried to run in to Dunkirk just before she sank. Area residents, including the keeper of the Dunkirk Light and his family, managed to salvage hundreds of bags of damp flour following the wreck. It is said that, when the flour dried out, it made perfectly good bread.

The loss of the freighter *Idaho* off Dunkirk, during the late fall of 1897, brought a different sort of bounty to the area. The ship was carrying a large load of merchandise intended to be sold as Christmas presents, including a hefty store of chocolate, which washed ashore in large slabs. No doubt children hereabouts had a very sweet Christmas that year.

Though a museum now resides in the keeper's house, the Dunkirk Light still shines across Lake Erie.

BARCELONA LIGHTHOUSE

T he Barcelona Lighthouse's claim to fame is its distinction as the first public building in the United States—and perhaps the only lighthouse in the world—to be illuminated by gas. The structure stands near a gas-emitting spring, so the experiment in using this alternative fuel source was a natural.

The lighthouse, built in 1829 on a bluff in Portland Harbor, as it was then called, had conventional oil lamps and a 14-inch reflector. Three years after it began operating, residents of this community made an astonishing discovery: a pool of water that would, on occasion, catch fire. This "burning spring" produced natural gas, which was soon piped to the tower and put to work guiding ships. The gas, burned in a specially designed lamp, produced a flame so intense that sailors on Lake Erie sometimes reported that the whole lighthouse seemed on fire. Sometime after 1838 the gas ran out and the Barcelona keeper had to replace the tower's original oil lamps.

In 1859 the lighthouse achieved another distinction, this one embarrassing. Government inspectors discovered that the station had been a mistake from the first. The light had been built to guide vessels into Barcelona's harbor, but Barcelona, as it turned out, had no harbor. The light was immediately discontinued.

Despite its short career the lighthouse survived and still stands today. Now a private residence, the 40-foot conical tower and its keeper's cottage are so attractive they are often depicted on postcards. The lantern was removed long ago, but a wooden framework at the top suggests the tower's original function.

TO SEE THE LIGHT: Located just off I–90 on East Lake Road (Route 5) in Barcelona, the lighthouse is a private residence not open to the public. The structure can be seen from the public right-of-way, but visitors are asked to please not trespass on the private property.

Location: Barcelona

Established: 1829

Tower height: 40 feet

Status: Deactivated 1859

Note: Early use of natural gas as an illuminant

GLOSSARY

Aids to Navigation Team

Coast Guard units assigned to operate and maintain lighthouses, channel lights, buoys, and other maritime markers.

Argand lamp

A clean-burning oil lamp widely used in lighthouses during the late eighteenth and early nineteenth centuries. Designed by French inventor Ami Argand, they produced an intense flame and a very bright light.

Automated light

A lighthouse with no keeper. Following World War II, remote control systems, light-activated switches, and fog-sensing devices made automation an increasingly cost-effective and attractive option, and the efficiency-minded Coast Guard automated one light station after another. By 1970, only about sixty U.S. lighthouses still had full-time keepers, and within two decades, all but one of those beacons had been automated.

Beacon

A light or radio signal intended to guide mariners or aviators.

Breakwater light

Often harbors are protected from high waves by a lengthy barrier of stone called a breakwater. Because they rise only a few feet above the surface, breakwaters are hard to see, especially at night, and may threaten vessels entering or exiting the harbor. Breakwater beacons are meant to make mariners aware of this hazard and safely navigate the harbor entrance. For obvious reasons, the light tower usually is placed near the end of the breakwater.

Bug light

From a distance, lighthouses built on piles in open water look a bit like water bugs floating on the surface, hence the nickname "bug light." However, some old-time mariners claim the bug lights got their name because of the enormous numbers of insects attracted by their beacons.

Caisson towers

During the late nineteenth century, the government began building offshore lighthouses on caissons. Essentially, a caisson was a hollow shell made of heavy, rolled-iron plates. Bolted together on land, the caisson was hauled to the construction site, sunk into the seabed up to a depth of about 30 feet, and then filled with sand, gravel, rock, or concrete.

Cast-iron towers

Introduced as a building material during the 1840s, cast iron revolutionized lighthouse construction. Stronger than stone and relatively light, cast iron made it possible to fabricate the parts of a light tower in a far-off foundry and then ship them to the construction site for assembly. A cylindrical structure assembled in 1844 on Long Island Head in Boston Harbor may have been the first all cast-iron lighthouse. The steel skeleton built at Coney Island still stands and serves mariners.

Characteristic

The identifying feature of a lighthouse beacon. To help mariners tell one beacon from another, maritime officials gave each light a distinct color or pattern of flashes. The information blocks in each lighthouse section provide characteristics of that particular beacon. Some are fixed, meaning that the light is on constantly during evening hours or in bad weather and does not flash. Other lights may flash at given intervals of, say, five, ten, or fifteen seconds. Still others may be green or red.

Clamshell or bivalve lenses

Most Fresnel lenses are round, but some have a slightly squeezed or flattened shape somewhat like that of a clamshell. They nearly always feature a pair of bull's-eyes or focal points, one on each side of the lens.

Coast Guard, U.S.

Since 1939, lighthouses and other aids to navigation in the United States have been the responsibility of the U.S. Coast Guard. Previously, the nation's maritime lights were maintained by a separate government agency known as the U.S. Lighthouse Service.

Elevation or height of the focal plane

Fresnel lenses and most modern optical systems channel light signals into a narrow band known as the focal plane. Since the curvature of the earth would render low-lying lights practically worthless for navigation, a coastal beacon must have an elevated focal plane. The height of the plane above the water's surface—usually from 40 to 200 feet—helps determine the range of the light.

Fixed signal

A lighthouse beacon that shines constantly during its regular hours of operation is said to display a "fixed" signal.

Flashing signal

A lighthouse beacon that turns on and off or grows much brighter at regular intervals is called a flashing signal.

Fog signal or foghorn

A distinct sound signal, usually a horn, trumpet, or siren, used to warn vessels away from prominent headlands or navigational obstacles during fog or other periods of low visibility.

Fresnel lenses

Invented in 1822 by Augustin Fresnel, a noted French physicist, Fresnel lenses concentrate light into a powerful beam that can be seen over great distances. Usually, they consist of individual hand-polished glass prisms arrayed in a bronze frame. Manufactured by a number of French or British companies, these devices came in as many as eleven different sizes or "orders." A massive first-order lens may be more than 6 feet in diameter and 12 feet tall, while a diminutive sixth-order lens is only about one foot wide and not much larger than an ordinary gallon jug.

Visitors to the Old Sodus Lighthouse can see this 3.5-order Fresnel lens in the tower.

Gallery

A circular walkway with a railing around the lantern of a lighthouse. Galleries provided keepers convenient access to the outside of the lantern for window cleaning, painting, and repair work.

Harbor light

A beacon intended to assist vessels moving in and out of a harbor. Not meant to serve as major coastal markers, harbor lights often consisted of little more than a lantern hung from a pole. However, many were official light stations with a tower and residence for the keeper. The Statue of Liberty once served as a harbor light.

Keeper

Before the era of automation, responsibility for operating and maintaining a light station was placed in the hands of a keeper, sometimes aided by one or more assistants. During the eighteenth and nineteenth centuries keepers were appointed by the Treasury Department or even the president himself in return for military service or a political favor. Although the work was hard and the pay minimal, these appointments were coveted since they offered a steady income and free housing.

Keeper's residence or dwelling

The presence of a keeper's residence is what turned a light station into a light "house." Sometime keepers lived in the tower itself, but a typical lighthouse dwelling was a detached one-and-a half-story wood or stone structure built in a style similar to that of other working-class homes in the area.

Lamp and reflector

For several decades prior to the introduction of the highly efficient Fresnel lens, lighthouse beacons were intensified by means of lamp-and-reflector systems. These combined a bright-burning lamp and a polished mirror shaped in a manner intended to concentrate the light.

Lantern

The glass-enclosed space at the top of a light tower is known as the lantern. It houses the lens or optic and protects it from the weather.

Lewis, Winslow

A former New England sea captain, Winslow Lewis built dozens of U.S. lighthouses during the first half of the nineteenth century. Lewis' bids for these projects were often quite low and the quality of the towers he built notoriously low. Lewis introduced his own version of the Argand lamp and reflector system—many considered it vastly inferior to the original. Most of New York's early light stations were at one time or another equipped with a Lewis optic.

Ironically, the diminutive Jeffrey's Hook Light is the only navigational tower in Manhattan.

Ronald J. Foster

Lighthouse

A term applied to a wide variety of buildings constructed for the purpose of guiding ships. Often it is used interchangeably with similar or derivative terms such as "light tower" or "light station." Throughout this book you will often find the more general term "light" used in reference to individual lighthouses or light stations.

Lighthouse Board

Beginning in 1851 and for more than half a century afterwards, U.S. lighthouses were administered by a Lighthouse Board consisting of nine members. Usually Board members were noted engineers, scientists, or military men. Creation of the Board brought a fresh professional spirit and penchant for innovation to the Lighthouse Service. Perhaps the Board's most telling change was adoption of the advanced Fresnel lens as the standard U.S. lighthouse optic.

Lighthouse Service

A common term applied to the various organizations or agencies that built and maintained U.S. lighthouses from 1789 until 1939 when the Coast Guard was placed in charge.

Lightships

Equipped with their own beacons, usually displayed from a tall central mast, lightships were essentially floating lighthouses. They marked shoals or key navigational turning points where construction of a permanent light tower was either impossible or prohibitively expensive.

Light station

A navigational facility with a light beacon is commonly referred to as a light station. Often the term is used interchangeably with "light-house," but a light station may or may not include a tower, quarters for a keeper, or a fog signal.

Light tower

A tall, often cylindrical structure used to elevate a navigational light so that mariners can see it from a distance. Modern light towers support a lantern, which houses a lamp, electric beacon, or some other lighting device. Some light towers are an integral part of the station residence, but most are detached.

Modern optic

A term referring to a broad array of lightweight, mostly weatherproof devices that produce the most modern navigational lights.

Occulting or eclipsing light

There are several ways to produce a beacon that appears to flash. One is to "occult" or block the light at regular intervals, often with a rotating opaque panel.

Pleasonton, Stephen

A parsimonious Treasury Department auditor, Pleasonton took charge of the Lighthouse Service in 1820 and maintained a firm if not stifling grip on it for thirty years. Most historians agree that Pleasonton's tightfistedness encouraged low construction standards and delayed U.S. adoption of the advanced optical technology for many years.

Private aid to navigation

A privately owned and maintained navigational light. Often, such lights are formerly deactivated beacons that have been reestablished for historic or aesthetic purposes.

Screw-pile towers

Open-water lighthouses built in rivers, bays, and other shallow water areas were often placed on piles that had been fitted with spiral flanges that made it possible to screw them into the subsurface sedimentary material. The screw piles often supported a lightweight wooden cottage with a small tower and lantern on its roof.

Skeleton towers

Iron- or steel-skeleton light towers consist of four or more heavily braced metal legs topped by workrooms and/or a lantern. Relatively durable and inexpensive, they were built in considerable numbers during the latter half of the nineteenth century. Since their open walls offer little resistance to wind and water, these towers proved ideal for offshore navigational stations, but some were built on land.

Solar-powered optic

Nowadays, many remote lighthouse beacons are powered by batteries recharged during the day by solar panels.

Sparkplug, teakettle, or coffeepot lights

Many open-water lighthouses in northern climates are built on round, concrete-filled caissons, which protect them from fast-flowing water and ice floes. Usually, the massive caissons are black while the cylindrical iron towers on top of them are painted white, giving them the appearance of an automobile spark plug. However, some think they look more like teakettles or coffeepots. The Orient Point tower is considered a coffeepot light.

Wickies

Before electric power made lighthouse work much cleaner and simpler, nearly all navigational beacons were produced by oil or kerosene lamps. Most of these lamps had wicks that required constant care and trimming. Consequently, lighthouse keepers often referred to themselves somewhat humorously as "wickies."

During Oswego's Harborfest, Fort Ontario puts on living history demonstrations complete with historical characters giving tours and doing Revolutionary War-era drills.

ABOUT THE AUTHORS

Photographs by **Bruce Roberts** have appeared in numerous magazines, including *Life* and *Sports Illustrated*, and in hundreds of books, many of them about lighthouses. He was director of photography at *Southern Living* magazine for many years. His work is also on display in the permanent collection at the Smithsonian Institution. He lives in Morehead City, North Carolina.

Ray Jones is the author or coauthor of fourteen best-selling books about lighthouses. He has served as an editor at Time-Life Books, as founding editor of *Albuquerque Living* magazine, as writing coach at *Southern Living* magazine, and as founding publisher of Country Roads Press. He lives in Pebble Beach, California, where he continues to write about lighthouses and serves as a consultant to businesses, publishers, and other authors.

ALSO BY BRUCE ROBERTS AND RAY JONES

Lighthouses of California
A Guidebook and Keepsake

Lighthouses of Florida
A Guidebook and Keepsake

Lighthouses of Maine
A Guidebook and Keepsake

Lighthouses of Michigan
A Guidebook and Keepsake

Lighthouses of Massachusetts
A Guidebook and Keepsake

Lighthouses of Washington
A Guidebook and Keepsake

Lighthouses of Wisconsin
A Guidebook and Keepsake

New England Lighthouses
Maine to Long Island Sound

American Lighthouses
A Comprehensive Guide

Eastern Great Lakes Lighthouses
Ontario, Erie, and Huron

Western Great Lakes Lighthouses
Michigan and Superior

Gulf Coast Lighthouses
Florida Keys to the Rio Grande

Mid-Atlantic Lighthouses
Hudson River to Chesapeake Bay

Pacific Northwest Lighthouses
Oregon, Washington, Alaska, and British Columbia

Southern Lighthouses
Outer Banks to Cape Florida